When I Was
Young and Old

Who can see the green earth any more
As she was by the sources of Time?

From "The Future," Matthew Arnold

When I Was
Young and Old

poems and prose

Freya Manfred

NODIN PRESS

Cover painting, I Am a Garden, by Freya Manfred.

ACKNOWLEDGMENTS

"When I Was Young And Old," Pensive: A Journal of Spirituality & the Arts, Issue #6, Spring 2023.

"Still Wild," "A Home Away From Home," "Ode to Indigo," "With the Dead at Blue Mound": Oakwood (South Dakota State University, Brookings, S.D.) Volume 5, Number 1, April 2023.

"I Wanted A Break": North Coast Review—A Poetry Harbor publication, Duluth, Minnesota, Issue #3, August 1993.

ISBN: 978-1-947237-51-3

9 8 7 6 5 4 3 2 1

Library of Congress Control Number: 2023933563

Published by

Nodin Press
210 Edge Place
Minneapolis, MN   55418
www.nodinpress.com

Printed in U.S.A.

For Tom, Bly, and Rowan Pope, who once again became my best readers and critics, and who are such fine artists in their own right.

And for Norton Stillman.

BY FREYA MANFRED

POETRY

A Goldenrod Will Grow

Yellow Squash Woman

American Roads

Flesh And Blood

My Only Home

The Blue Dress

Swimming With A Hundred Year Old Snapping Turtle

Speak, Mother

Loon In Late November Water

MEMOIR

Frederick Manfred: A Daughter Remembers

Raising Twins: A True Life Adventure

CONTENTS

When I Was
Young and Old

Art like prayer is a hand outstretched in the darkness, seeking for some touch of grace which will transform it into a hand that bestows gifts.

— Franz Kafka

Writing Poems and Reading Them Aloud

TRUST THE words. No, not just the words – trust the letters. Stand in the shadow of T. Sit in the lap of C. Take a wild ride on S. Fall into V or U. The longer you swim within the wonderful O, the more you realize the world is made of O's. Don't worry about the audience, or yourself, standing in front of them, naked or nervous. Allow the sound, the feeling, and the meaning of each letter and word to pass through your body into the audience. Relax, because this moment is about the words and their song.

When I sit by a lake to write, words come to me from the lake, through the lake, and because of the lake; and when I read a poem, the words move through me into the audience. I am merely the link between two worlds. The world of words and the world of nature are older, larger places, containing a wilderness of possibility, both beautiful and dangerous. Reader and audience can disappear together into the magic of words just as we disappear into the magic of nature, and all a writer or reader need do is let the magic be heard and felt.

Poems bridge the distance between people. Poems bring us closer to our sorrow and our joy. Poems want to be touched, gnawed, kicked, or kissed, and they prefer to be devoured raw, even if they are bitter, sour, or full of tears. Poems need readers and listeners drunk on words – words that make us feel lost, wild, angelic, or devilish – words that rock us to sleep in their mothering, fathering arms.

So, poet, speak!

IN A SAD TIME WHAT DO I DESIRE?

I want to laugh a liquid laugh,
every gurgling morsel of me
cascading like water over singing stones –

laugh until my heart and lungs are empty,
and go on laughing until I'm well-fed
and fall in love with everything –

let go of my place, and my body in that place,
and surrender to nonstop giggles, gasps,
chortles and chuckles –

laugh until I cry, and discover
the sapphires tumbling from my eyes are tears
rising from a deep sea of hope and sorrow.

Laugh! Because the more I remember
and then forget, the more I will be free.

I

STILL WILD

When I Was Young and Old

Out of nowhere we found ourselves
stretched out under the sun on the summer lawn,
and I saw how lively, how supple, he was
in each new pose, as I breathed in, *yes*, and out *yes*,

and when we sat down to eat I heard every word
he spoke, *yes*, as if he knew I would always understand,
and I asked for soup that was green and wild,
and he wanted to taste it, and I said *yes* again,

and on the mountains we slid so smoothly
through snow drifts, down icy-steep ravines,
on our two simple, matter-of fact feet, *yes* –
and when I wandered off alone,
the wolf who followed us did not attack,
but went his solitary way, so I felt safe, *yes*.

And when we lay down together, at last,
I was amazed how much care he gave
to my humble, forgotten ears and cosmic toes,
and when he kissed me, I slipped like lightning
into another world, *yes* and *yes* and *yes*.

This all happened when he was young and I was old,
and I was young and he was old,
and it still happens whenever a dream arrives at night
to assure me it was all meant to be.

But now I wonder, is my dream more alive
than the poem I write about the dream?
And is my life as alive, as real, as the poem or the dream?

Yes, and *yes*, and *yes*.

STILL WILD

I long to live in a house by a lake
with a man whose hands are warmer than my own,

to walk with him on the moss and mushroom path,
picking berries, the sun on our shoulders,

to listen to the owl hoot-hooting in the night
and imagine her listening, watching, waiting,

and then the swooping flight and raw devouring
that promises death, and new life.

I long to see two golden eagles share a giant fish,
and then fly away, one east, one west,

birds who embody the freedom and courage
I try to summon when I worry about the ones I love,

all of them hopefully asleep now, within dreams
that will sustain them when they wake.

I long to walk down to the lake that welcomes me
with quicksilver calm and untamed fury.

Because I am wild, still wild, and this is where I belong.

A Home Away from Words

I slip my lanky self into the silver-smiling lake
    and swim along the shore
to watch the lakeweed sway, green and grey,
    and swarming, fleeting fish
the size of sardines and salad plates.

I stop to rest on a rock shaped like a mushroom,
    slick with hairy green moss,
where I try to stand until I slide off
    and stroke back through pondweed
sprouting up from the darkness below
    where dead trees lie,
sodden, broken, and studded with shells.

In the distance I see my love on shore,
    reading, and watching out for me.
He knows I have a yearning sadness in my heart
    that eases when I swim on and on
without thinking, into the arms of the woman
    I become, caressed by water,
my home away from words.

FREE SWIMMER

When I swim out into the lake
      and travel the ancient waterways

the shifting current embraces me and convinces me
      that I have fins and a tail

and that I'm stronger and more supple
      than I will ever be on land.

Everything's suddenly so clear.
      I don't need or want anyone.

They're welcome to join me,
      but it's sweeter if they don't.

I don't want any thing, either,
      since everything is here, fresh and fishy,

cool and warm, sparkling and somber,
      with the oldest colors and shapes on earth,

each a flowing part of where and who I am –
      now, and long ago, and in times to come.

I am not any one, or any thing,
      and yet I've never felt so sure of my next move.

In a Dream I Turn into Myself

Think of that. Being alive with a girl
Who could turn into a laurel tree
Whenever she felt like it.
                    — James A. Wright

At a poetry reading in a tree-filled park
each poet was granted five minutes to perform.

I sat on a folding chair in the last row
listening to lush, crooning cadences,
seismic stanzas where fate rode on every word,
and loquacious lyrics that dwindled into drool.

Hours later, weary of watching poets
watch other poets read,
I tipped my chair back into the grass
and lay staring up into clouds, birds,
and the beckoning green tops of trees,

and soon I flew away with my whole heart
and more than half my mind and soul
and turned back into myself.

ODE TO INDIGO

My deepest desire
is to ride the rainbow
into indigo,
that silken source of light
streaming toward me
from the beginning of creation,
pure indigo! –
where I find iridescent images,
resounding cadences,
words I can't regret,
and embrace the truth
that flies toward me
from the wild indigo distance.

Then I'll rest my bones
in shades of green,
lying across fields and forests,
dig in with fingers and toes
to smell the growing, twining mosses,
microbes, and mysteries
who feed me
while I muse and meditate –
until I rise up again to sing a song
I hope will last as long as desire –
as long as indigo.

DORECHO DREAM

Dorecho: a wide-spread, damaging thunderstorm.

In this dream I arrive on time,
fully dressed for once,
but when they ask me to speak,
I've left my poems at home again
with no time to retrieve them.
I have nothing to say, no words
to make my thoughts and feelings clear.
My body, without blood, flesh, or bone,
flattens like a flimsy paper doll.

I sometimes write from wherever love,
hate, courage, and kindness lie,
but even in this recurring dream
I'm too often lost in my own home,
bumbling from room to room,
trying to survive the daily mysteries.

When I wake, I ask, *What is my hope?*
To grow apples? To climb a mountain?
To swim naked in a welcoming sea?

Or maybe, just to *be*.

Before the After, After the Before

He was dead slick keen,
the man in my dream last night,
lanky legs white in the moonlight,
black in the lake light, blue in the starlight,
green in the forest light,
and I knew he'd always be with me –
before the after, and after the before.

He was a real man and a made up man,
and in the middle of our longed-for night,
our old night, our young night,
our forever beloved night,
I felt as safe as first love, as last love,
as never or forever love,
with nowhere, and everywhere, to go.

Just us, whoever we were, whoever we are,
real, or imagined, or both.
Call it marriage or call it luck –
it's what we lived through and live through,
what we invented and invent
with all our power and weakness,
but can never control or understand.

And in the long run and the short run –
all last night, in every kind of light –
the man in my dream was dead, slick, keen.

II

THE LILAC HOUSE

THE LILAC HOUSE

EVERY YEAR IN late May and early June dozens of lilacs around our house bloomed white, purple, and many shades of lavender. Dad said the lilac bushes were planted by previous owners who ordered them decades ago from England and France. Many had grown as tall as trees, and all of them had beautiful heart-shaped leaves. Between our house and Doctor Beach's house there was one bank of lilacs that stood as wide and almost as high as the First National Bank in Oxboro, a nearby village which later became part of Bloomington. And in this green, heaven-perfumed cloud of lilacs I decided to build myself a Lilac House.

I didn't touch the thick trunks of the lilac trees, which were sometimes six to ten inches in diameter, but I cut the flexible, almost-rubbery lilac branches down to ground level so I could walk along a network of paths that I cleared of leaves. Some paths were dead ends and others led to a few dirt-floored rooms. At one end of my Lilac House I carved out a living room and a pantry where I stored peanut butter and crabapples in some jars I took from our kitchen. Behind the pantry, in the thickest part of the bushes, I made several small round bedrooms, scraping dead leaves into piles and depositing them along the sides of each room. Here and there, I stuck dried flowers and garden herbs into tin cans for decoration. My paths zigzagged and took unexpected turns into tiny, secret rooms where I made "picture window lookouts" with scenic views of the neighbors' houses and the surrounding countryside. Every day my Lilac House changed its shape and size, depending on the work I did with my bare hands.

Not far from my Lilac House an even larger stand of very tall lilacs had grown up between Doctor Beach's flower garden and our vegetable garden, so I decided I would construct a Lilac City. I built a wide Main Street, with a store, a post office, and a tiny leafy throne-room in City Hall for myself, Queen of Lilac City. I was wary about colonizing my Lilac City at first because it lay near the field where Doctor Beach's son, Joe Beach, played baseball with his buddies, and there was no telling when they might discover it and trample it with their boy-energy. I strewed leaves around the front and back entrances of my Lilac City so the boys wouldn't notice the well-swept path that led to Main Street. I had to be very careful because Joe's younger brother, Nemo, who had contracted polio, lived very close to the ground when he decided to crawl around the yard instead of using his crutches. But even Nemo never detected my Lilac City.

Only a few neighborhood dogs found me in my Lilac House or my Lilac City. My favorite dog was Wagner, a large, lanky golden retriever, who belonged to Joe and Nemo. Mrs. Beach told me she named Wagner for the composer, but I called him "Wags" because his tail always welcomed me. He was young and malleable, a bit like my siblings, so by giving him a few table scraps I was able to convince him to play with me instead of running off with some of his dog friends. Our favorite game was Battleground of the Dinosaurs, which we played on Main Street, though Wags preferred to call our game Never Let Go. Head down, eyes glowering, Wags growled at me, stretching his black lips back from his white prong teeth, which were firmly planted in my old winter scarf. Using his teeth and all his muscles he pulled as hard as he could in one direction while I pulled in the other. Ears flapping, tail spinning, neck jerking, Wags stalked backward, even when I pretended to snarl to scare him. Slowly but very surely he dragged me toward his end of Main Street because he was, finally, stronger than I was. And according to my rules that meant he had won our game. I never won. We both knew that I could only win if I persuaded him to release his toothy grip, and I never could, unless I gave him a treat.

Wags also played Never Let Go with the toys that I hid from him. I'd sit in one of my secret rooms reading *Alice's Adventures in Wonderland* and laughing to my heart's content when Alice said, "I'm not a mile high!" and the King said, "You are," and the Queen added, "Nearly two miles high." and I'd get a delightful ghosty feeling that Wags was up to something new, snuffing up and down the leafy hallways. When the reason for his search finally dawned on me, it was always too late. He'd already found one of my treasures and opened his big toothy trap and engulfed it, and there he stood across the room, his eyes wide with challenge, rolling something around in the brine of his mouth.

"Whatcha got, Wags? C'mon! Show me!" I put my book down slowly and then tried to grab him before he turned tail and ran into one of the corridors. Drooling mightily, he pranced backward, grinding his molars, "Arrrrrrrg."

"Wags! Give me that ball!" I tried to grab the collar around his neck, but he feinted and ran away. Like a mad bomber he thrashed through one room after the next, leaves exploding and flying around him. Boisterous, berserk, he systematically helped me wreck the new borders of my house until I gave up and fell down panting.

I laid there, staring up at the blue sky through the green leaves until Wags crept up beside me and leaned on me, his cool wet nose snorkeling my arm pits and my crotch, still drooling around the greenish-grey thing in his mouth. "Arrrf!" he said. Which meant, "Don't give up so easily."

Now I could see exactly which treasure he had stolen. "That's my very newest tennis ball!" It looked like a wet rat wedged between his teeth.

"ARRRG," he growled, low and ecstatic, which meant, "You know very well it's my ball, not yours."

And then he let me pry at his teeth with my fingers until I rose to my full height and towered over him like a Queen. "You give me that tennis ball! It's brand new. And you're a bad dog!"

Wags hung his head, rolling his eyes up like periscopes to stare at me, still clenching the wet ball with every tooth. "Grrr," he said, which meant, "Make me."

I usually gave up and went back to reading my book. But within moments Wags inevitably minced up to me, ball wedged in his teeth, his hot breath blooming across my face.

When he finally realized I was really, truly, not going to play anymore, he gently dropped the wet ball on a pile of leaves, flopped down with his back wedged against me, and sighed deeply. He closed his eyes while I read aloud from Alice, Huckleberry Finn, or The Selected Poems of Emily Dickinson. I enjoyed changing my voice for each character. I crooned as the Cheshire Cat or yelled and cackled crazily with the whisky-sobbing voice of Huck's drunken pap. But Wags seemed to prefer Emily because when I read her poems he never took his eyes off me for long: a needy brother, sister, and friend, rolled into one.

I always felt entirely safe from all the world snuggling with Wags in my Lilac House, inhaling his muddy, sunny-haired dog smell, and stroking his soft fur. "Dear old Wags!" I whispered, and he knew what I meant.

III

SWIMMING IN
THE DARK

SWIMMING IN THE DARK

In my dream my love and I are suddenly swimming
    in the dark,
and I wonder how much I can trust myself to the sea

with only a few points of light on land to remind us
how far we've drifted from our familiar shore.

We've floated under the stars for years, lucky to be together,
neither too frightened nor too brave to carry on,

but now we're rocked by great, heaving, nameless swells
stretching far beyond our fragile selves.

When did the waves begin to sing of constant danger
to remind us that we could be lost to each other forever?

Was it when we could no longer hear the words of dying
friends above the roar of silence?

Or was it when we stopped trusting our love,
and could no longer follow our hearts into the wilderness?

When I wake, I will try to find my way back
to calmer waters and the reassuring lights on shore.

We must go on until we can no longer see, hear, speak,
or weather our lives together, and bear what's true.

I Ask My Heart

I ask my heart why it trembles, but there's no reply.

An invisible wall divides me from myself,
and the flow of love that answers love has slowed.

I need to trust my heart, but I quake with fear
when I remember the pain that love can cause.

After years of trying to embrace what I have, and accept
what I do not, I wonder if I was ever just alone, and free?

Oh yes, I was thirteen, rocking on the porch swing, reading
stacks of books, dreaming I would wander the world,

a breathless, curious observer, submerged in creation,
where shape, sound, smell, taste, and touch is enough,

along with gratitude for being born, falling in love,
and surviving with a whole heart.

Near You

My constant desire is for closeness. Now.
Before the setting sun lights the far shore for the last time.

I want to share fleeting and long lasting truths,
newly discovered or left unspoken long ago –

truths told in plain words, worth more than facts
and figures, or dazzling speeches.

I crave a conversation as fresh as a swallow of water
with an enduring spirit that keeps us alive –

something to believe in, even when we tell the truths
we sometimes fear to hear.

Shared true-heart moments are the light of this universe.
They tell us what we do here on earth is all that matters,

because we meet death every day
if we have no truths to hold close, or give away.

Talking Tough

Don't visit my dreams, even with your sweetest face
or wearing your favorite clothes. Rest inside your own dreams.

Don't wait for me to ask you to stay strong and healthy.
Just take a walk down that yearning, beckoning road.

Don't look for safety in my house or in my bed.
There's no one here who will always give you what you want.

Very few people help me keep my peace of mind,
and those who do don't believe their own songlike serenity.

That's the gift they give and the gift I hope to give –
to offer peace to others without worrying how it's given.

It ought to be a natural motion, a rising, falling wave,
a cloud flowing in the wind, inventing itself as it goes,

the way blue herons fly all day and night across this lake
feeding insects and fish to their young.

Sometimes they fly so close to shore I can feel
their time-weathered profiles in my ancient bones.

ARCHEGOSAURUS

I often wander the woods at dusk, and remember
how a river never forgets its beginnings or endings,
its dark underground springs or bright singing waterfalls.

When a startled toad leaps away from me
the slimed leather of its skin reminds me of a creature
with a cavernous mouth and jagged teeth
who waited to devour me on the dark path to our home
when I was only five or six.

Years later, I found a postcard of an Archegosaurus
who looked like my hungry monster, head to toe,
and like no other dinosaur I'd ever seen.

How did I conjure up this prehistoric amphibian
who lived three hundred million years ago?
And why did it threaten me when I tried so hard
to become the well-behaved child I was asked to be?
Was I too young to save my growing soul
from the rage and grief adults expressed when I could not?

Now I walk the woods at dusk,
no longer burdened by the fear of being devoured.
I greet the ancient creature inside me, and I know its name.

THE WINDOW BY THE LAKE

I wake before dawn above our beloved lake
and wait for the sun to join me.

Stalwart cedars stand silent, their black arms silhouetted
against the softly heaving water.

Two does and a fawn arrive to crop the grass near shore,
their bodies outlined against the waves.

Not far away a shaggy animal very much like a wolf
gnaws a long white bone.

And this wolf, if it is a wolf, is more than I can believe,
so at home, wild-eyed, and waiting.

And look! Far off, the wide blue sky trumpets into view.
The end of darkness. If not the beginning of light.

At Seventy, He Plants a Tree

After we chose a tree, he dug a hole,
first with a shovel, then with his bare hands,
through dirt, clay, and rocks as big as fists
kneeling on a scrap of cardboard to protect his knees,
sweat streaming down his gritty shirt.

And after he set the little cedar in place,
surrounded the roots with black soil,
and watered, and watered again, he stood up
and came inside, groaning, but also sighing-happy,
and drew off his sodden clothes and showered
and stretched out on our bed and fell asleep.

And everything he'd done to plant that tree
to guard our north-facing front door
was so arduous I could not do it myself –
not anymore, now that I'm only good for a stroll,
a languid swim, or cooking soup for dinner.

I felt as if he'd finally given birth,
when so far I've always been the only mother here.
I thought that tree was close to a miracle,
and I showed it to our sons, who were pleased,
even proud. They nodded and approved
as if they were our doting parents.

I could see they planned to plant their own trees,
like their father, this hardy man in league with earth,
air, water, and the hard-earned promise of growth.
It terrified me. To see how strong some people can be.
I can only celebrate by loving all of them
with every bit of wrinkled bark and sweet sap
left in my aging brain and veins.

Some Other Train, Some Other Dream

I dreamed I took an open-topped train
to explore a wild green land I could see in the distance,

but the train stopped at a bridge over a ravine
and the engineer warned me it was dangerous to go on.

I saw a stream at the bottom that flowed through grass
and flowers, and I wondered if I could go on alone, on foot.

Instead, I took a bus with a hot-foot driver back to town,
until I realized I'd left my purse on the train.

A stranger lent me his phone to call my husband,
who drove to the train to find my purse.

I was lucky to avoid a bad accident on that train,
lucky to meet a kind stranger,

and lucky to have a loving husband –
though I missed the new country I had hoped to see.

And now I wait for some other train, some other time,
some other dream, to travel my way.

A Not Unwelcome Peace

At times I can't remember where we were or where we are,
or who I was, or who I am now.

Once I held your hand, and my body cried *hello!* But now
you feel too familiar when you're near.

My heart doesn't flutter as it once did, and little we say
leads to much more than two steaming cups of tea.

A bird sings a song in an ancient tree, and our cat climbs
to the top and comes down with nothing in her claws.

Given my passionate past, the present surprises me, drifting
quietly in a mist – but it's not an unwelcome peace.

The animal I was drowses toward sleep, but not a final sleep,
as I lie, forever purring, beside you in the sun.

THE UNBELIEVABLE – A POEM FOR TOM

I'm free to make mushroom soup
if you're not there to eat it.

Free to lie down beside a blue flower
if you can't see or smell it.

Free to climb up or down the mountain
without your helping hand.

Free to hear and feel the thunder
if it runs along my spine.

Free not to care if I lose track
of our decades-long journey.

And free to stop breathing
if you're not here to feel my breath.

I thought I had a leaping imagination,
but this dreadful freedom

is as unbelievable as your death.

Writing in the Dark

The sun goes down and evening comes on,
but the world still beckons, near to far, far to near,
in layers of darkness and light.

Black ducks rise in V-formations
and fly across the lake's last silver ripples
until they're almost out of sight, and then a surprise –

they turn and fly over my head, honking and blaring,
while behind me the evening train clamors savagely,
until it, too, fades away and is gone.

A liquid apricot light soars up beyond the western hills
and sings to me like a clear-voiced clarinet,
a shy flute, a dreaming harp.

The distant music settles slowly into night,
but I keep writing on pages fading from white, to grey,
to black, until my last words are written in the dark,

though I can no longer see.

IV

GRAMMA SHORBA

Gramma Shorba

GRAMMA'S NAME WAS Mary Shorba and she was Mom's
mother. She lived on the bottom floor of a duplex near
the University of Minnesota, and as far as I could see she
loved every single thing I ever said or did. She never made
me feel guilty or too young or too old or too mad or too
sad. She said she couldn't get enough of me and that she
was "happy as a lark" when I came to stay because I always
helped her look for her eyeglasses and ran errands when
her legs were hurting. "I have trouble walking because a
car ran over me and broke nearly every bone in my body
when your mom was only two," Gram said. She pulled
up her dress to show me the crescent-shaped scars on
the insides of her knees. "I was laid up in the hospital for
six months. And in all that time I didn't set eyes on your
mother, my darling Maryanna. She had to go and live with
my parents."

"Couldn't she come and visit you in the hospital?"

"Young children were barred from hospitals in those
days. Because of diseases. When I got out, your Mom didn't
recognize me at first."

"Why did the car run over you?"

"Why? Gracious me! A bunch of men were driving
around drunk, and they started whistling and yelling at
me as I was walking along the sidewalk. I kept walking
and tried to ignore them, but the driver ran his car over
the curb and knocked me flat. Lord Above! My bones were
sticking out through my shins."

So when Gramma and I ventured into the city, we

avoided long walks and rode streetcars as much as possible because Gramma's right leg was bowed out and her left leg was bent too far forward, so she walked all cockeyed, rocking back and forth like a boat on rough water.

Sometimes, lying curled back to back with Gramma under the soft flannel sheets on the old brown couch she made into a bed at night, I wondered what my life would have been like if Gramma had died when the car full of drunken men hit her. Then I imagined my five foot one inch Gramma lying under the heavy wheels, bones sticking out of her shins and rivers of blood pouring from her heart. Gramma had never actually mentioned blood pouring from her heart, but that was the image I had as I fell asleep with my eyes fixed on a tiny red cloth heart hanging on a red ribbon that was draped over the corner of a photo of Gramma's only son, George Shorba. George had died in a motorcycle accident a few days after his fifteenth birthday. Gramma and I looked at his photo every night before bed, and after a moment of silent, heavy breathing, Gramma's tears began rolling down her cheeks onto the front of her nightgown. "He was my dear, sweet boy. And so my heart is broken. Broken forever. But I'm so thankful every day that you and Marya and Freddy are whole and healthy. Jesus loves little girls like you, but He shouldn't take you away like he took George."

"Why did Jesus take George?"

"Because George was always too good for this world, God forgive me."

"Forgive you for what? You didn't kill George."

"No, but he begged me for a birthday motorcycle, and I bought it for him – the instrument of his passing. I can only pray for forgiveness. May God help me and forgive me."

"God already loves you," I said. "So he has to forgive you. So don't worry! When you're sad you can come and visit me in my Lilac House. You can stay as long as you want. With me and Waggles."

"Waggles?"

"The Beachs' dog. He's one of my best friends, and so are you."

"Oh my," Gramma said, and she burst into tears again and started to laugh at the same time. It was great. I was so happy she cried and laughed at the same time whenever she felt like it, because then, of course, I could do the same thing whenever I wanted.

Gramma hugged and kissed me, then turned her face to the wall and began to snore. I could feel her back quivering against mine, and her loving heart beating less than a foot away from my healthier, younger heart. I fell asleep praying to every god and imaginary being I'd ever heard of – Jesus, Wakantonka, Buddha, Peter Pan, and all the elves and fairies who lived in the woods and waters – to make Gramma feel better. I hoped they would all get together to find a way to mend my Gramma's heart.

V

ROOTS AND RAINBOWS

GIVING BIRTH TO OUR SONS
WITH THE HELP OF EIGHT MEN

The night our sons were born
nothing and no one could stop me
from laughing or weeping
until I fell asleep
and dreamed I was in labor,
and eight rainbow-colored men
came up out of the earth to join me.

And when I gave birth
in a bath of scarlet blood
the men took hold of the babies
and lifted them high,
offering them to earth, moon, and sun,
so they might take root and grow,
under the wandering stars.

The men chanted and sang
without apology or rivalry,
all breathing the same free air
and dancing a rainbow dance
to honor the truth
of a woman giving birth.

OUR BETTER ANGELS

Do they sleep beside us while we sleep,
or do they lie wide-eyed under the scattered stars,
like the weary mother who has sung her children to sleep
and turns her face toward the beckoning leaves
of the darkening trees at the edge of the forest?

Her thoughts drift into the undergrowth
until she's no longer mother, woman, or angel –
but someone who can vanish into the vanishing day
and disappear, as we all disappear into moments
that plunge us into a new kind of being and becoming.

Who knows what lies within us?
Our solitary musings are a never-ending
beginning-of-life and end-of-life mystery,
as much a part of us as the mother, the woman,
or those deeply imagined better angels.

And, oh, here comes the evening wind – a sacred breath,
rising from heaven and earth to round out the world.

I Wanted a Break

I wanted a break from parenting,
and from years of laundry, cooking, cleaning,
chopping, weeding, shouting, and compromising,
so I hopped a plane to see old friends.

First stop was a deli in New York City with Bea and Lou,
where I laughed myself under the table
describing how Tom and I scheme, in separate silence,
to pack and leave forever,
he in a new red Porsche, me in an old green Jeep.
I described our hallucinations due to sleep loss
while raising our infant twins,
and how for two years I stormed out of
every business establishment between LA and Frisco
because no one could wait on me fast enough
or with enough motherly concern.

In response I heard of Lou's infidelities,
Bea's loss of faith, Lou's drunken father,
Bea's dying mother, Lou's anorexic slut of a sister,
and the drugs they take for anxiety,
high blood pressure, sleeping, and waking.
Also how Bea left her last four jobs and hates the fifth,
and how their teenage children and closest friends
are drunks, punks, or have moved to Memphis.

Two days later, in Boston, Sue greeted me
with a diagram of her third marriage:
herpes, impotence, and no jokes.
Her ex-husband still breaks into her apartment
to smash furniture and her new husband's arms,
especially since their dog was poisoned.
Sue's breath is always short,
and she can't ride in cars, unless she drives,

and even then she spends hours fighting panic
and gaining weight at Burger King.

I was dying to get to Denver to see Joe and Cindi,
who found me in the airport bar.
By the time I climbed into the unmade bed in their attic,
I knew they'd never stay together past New Year's.
I also knew their dog was deeply depressed,
their cat would survive by moving to the neighbors,
and Joe's chain-smoking crazy-ass freeway driving
would cause his early death.

Joe and Cindi and I also discussed the arms race,
acid-filled lakes, condos swallowing cornfields,
how every movie nowadays is either deformed
from the start or crippled in the last act,
how apples and peaches don't taste the way they used to,
and how no one can afford a house,
let alone a new car, or a weekend in Vegas,
or do anything about the local schools and jails,
not to mention mental institutions.

Hell, we covered it all,
and I flew home two days early
just to add a few laughs
to my life.

DINNER WITH OUR SONS

We drink in the keen eyes, dark eyebrows, and deep cadences
of the two beloved men across from us at the table.

We rejoice in their leaping brains and the rich humor
that echoes generations buried not so many miles away.

We lean eagerly, gratefully, into our future and their future,
wondering how long we can remain beside them,

navigating this wild river with no wish to reach the unknown
country from which no one returns. "Not yet!" we say.

Our family works hard, pencils to paper, brushes to canvas,
songs, stories, pictures, and poems in our hearts –

but tonight we're wrapped in a sacred rhythm, each word part
of a precious symphony of sharing dinner with our sons.

When the Party's Over

We finish our chocolate desserts, and wave goodbye,
and open the door to rain that greets and greens the grass,

and the warm, lively rooms disappear behind us,
redolent with the aroma of human flesh, firewood, perfume,

and the lingering voices of family and friends
who longed to see us, just as we longed to see them.

We start our car and take the curve of the road right, then left,
then on to the freeway and the city lights,

the two of us traveling alone again, our future a mystery,
as the evening ebbs and flows and floods our brains

with a perfect chaos of conversation and memories
that sing to whoever we were before the party began.

HIGH SCHOOL FRIENDS

Seven women in their seventies gather on a restaurant patio
in the thrall of spring, shoulders stooped, hair going grey,
sharing healthy salads and pancakes steeped in syrup.

As we speak, our faces ignite, and vivid images rush and flow –
a new part-time job, a trip to Alaska, a good library book,
a serious operation, a garden full of cabbages and tomatoes.

Then the first death – a beloved husband, the sweeping grief,
the tear-washed face cleansed of hope and joy, but born again
with a dream we all share, a new grandchild coming soon.

Who will die next? Me? My beloved? You? Or yours?
And what do we truly know or feel about dying, even as death
embraces us from all sides and guides us through our days?

I don't know if we trust each other enough to share the terrors
and truths of life, but we do feel the joy and comfort
of long friendships that bind us together in the face of trouble.

We strolled the halls of our small town school together,
young faces full of fervor, books held tight to our chests,
bones growing as swiftly as our shifting desires and dreams.

And because we knew each other then, once and for all,
we feel safe for the moment, in each other's welcoming arms.

AFTER LOSING A FRIENDSHIP

Where am I when someone I love says goodbye?
Should I swallow more wine and wonder if I'm worth loving?

Do I no longer live where I was born, in a land that
breathed in and out to welcome me?

Should I worry that I was too silly, too bold, too shy,
or just too ripe with rage and thrashing sorrow?

Did I forget to compliment the cook, praise the musicians,
or bow to the kings and queens of wit?

Sometimes I can't keep up no matter how fast I grow.

But if I want to belong, my task is to take it all in, and dream
with friends who are lethally silly and deadly serious,

who will skate on thin ice with me, sharing secrets for free
in a wide, weird, wondrous world.

EXPECT NOTHING

I must learn to expect nothing of myself or anyone else
or I'll wear away to nothing,

and then I might surprise myself with all I have to give,
a hand up a hill, a caring voice.

With every wound life inflicts in a screaming void
you'd receive my embrace, free of burdens.

Expecting nothing from myself seems the best answer
to the endless diseases and wars wending toward us.

I need time to heal in the soothing balm of sleep,
free of the helpless desire to please the ones I love most,

who are hopefully wise and lucky enough to have learned
to expect nothing.

IN DREAMS I STAND MY GROUND

I long to feel safe from bombs in the mailbox,
screams at the door, and suicides in the bath.

I'm sick of lies, illusions, and delusions,
the fears that attack and invade my sleep.

I sometimes struggle to believe that I exist,
that I am heard, or have something to offer.

I yearn for peace, so I defend myself
by dreaming my way past anger or annihilation.

In dreams I refuse to be treated as if I'm invisible.
In dreams I speak up, and stand my ground.

How to Find a New Friend

Don't forget how lost you felt when your old friends died,
and try to believe in laughter again.

Don't think too long and hard about anything, or brood
about what you remember, or forget.

Whether you feel joy, sadness, anger, or fear, move closer
until you feel breath like music on your skin,
and peace in your heart, where food and shelter live.

Help others when you can, and let them help you.
And don't worry about heaven or hell –
it's what you do and say here that matters most.

If you travel my way, don't trust that I'm good with words.
They have escaped me all my life,
and I can't speak or write as clearly as I wish.

I hope that before I die, I'll find time to float in a lake
with the ones I love,
saying nothing that hasn't already been said.

Animal Soul

Last night I looked for a way to defeat the dreams
that make my poor heart drum with dread.

But at midnight we woke to screams outside the window
where our sweet young cat was crying for help.

Had a great horned owl snatched her with its talons?
Had the neighbor's demon cat slashed a new gash in her ear?

We ran toward her shrieks and stumbled onto the deck,
and out in the dark some thing huffed once – twice –

three times – and a shape like a fox or a wolf –
who could tell? – charged across the lawn –

and then at the top of a tall oak tree we saw our cat,
still wailing, as a white-tailed deer vanished into the woods.

When we called, she skinned slowly down, headfirst,
then tail first, then flew to join us, swift and safe and free.

And that night my dreaded dreams were gone – all gone –
banished by my leap from sleep to save another animal soul.

Helpful Ghosts

Lichen star-bursts, gold, grey and olive green,
are etched on the hoary rocks near the ravine
where our cat hunts for mice and moles.

Towering cottonwoods twelve feet thick
with deeply wrinkled skin too dense for hatchets
flutter their heart-shaped leaves in the slightest wind.

Grandma Shorba carries sweet corn in her apron,
hobbling from the garden to the house on scarred legs,
broken long ago by a careless, drunken driver.

South of the house, sun-blasted fence posts
march uphill and down, standing tall and straight
in holes dug by our hard-working father.

And in the kitchen mother's sun-brown hands
knead the dough for plum and apple pies
to share with our friends and neighbors.

This land is inhabited by haunting images and echoes
of the people I loved, who remind me to celebrate
the gifts of those who embraced us, supported us,

and saved us, so we could live here long enough
to put down roots, and set our children free.

Her Beauty

I followed my mother everywhere and found mystery —
peace and chaos, cold shock and heavenly awe.

Dark and defiant as night, sweet and tender as day,
I found her at the grand piano, swaying, singing sadly,

"In the mission of Saint Augustine, we said farewell,
and we made a vow to meet again, as teardrops fell ..."

I found her kneeling in the garden, gathering strawberries
still warm from the sun to share with me.

I found her in bed, musing, "Let's read Emily's poems,
heart to heart, *I like to see it lap the miles* ..."

Beautiful coming in from the wind and the rain,
beautiful at parties, welcoming friends and neighbors,

beautiful because our proud father said she was beautiful,
and because our wise grandma said she was beautiful,

and because I told myself she was beautiful
beyond anyone I had ever dreamed of, seen, or known.

She tried to hide her family secrets from all of us,
but we saw the shadows cross her face,

the waves of grief and fear that did not drown her,
as she held three besotted little lovers so bravely in her arms.

LAST ROSE OF SUMMER

My mother never forgot to celebrate
    and mourn the last rose of summer.
She held it out to me with a wistful smile
    so I could inhale the happiness
mixed with sadness in her voice,
    "Look, the last rose!"

I bowed to the soft petals and sharp thorns,
    to the immensity of that shared moment.
Years later, I still see her eyes,
    open to beauty,
yet forever shaded with sorrow,
    most sentient and beautiful mother.

We endured our bumbling tangles and jousts,
    our painful wondering
about what we meant or didn't mean to say.
    But we never forgot the last rose,
breathing softly in its slim glass vase
    until it lost its glory and folded itself away.

The last rose of summer is a promise and a regret,
    a reward, a warning, and a thorny truth.
It is a curious child, a ripening adult,
    and an aged and dying woman.
It is a mother's gift, precious as one moment –
    one breath in, and out.

Nemo

Nemo never complained. He used his powerful arms
to drag his withered legs into the oak and elm tree woods
where we built a secret fort with fallen branches
and hoarded hard green crabapples for battle
in case his brother, Joe, mounted a sneak attack.

At the end of each day we drank cherry Kool-Aid
and watched *The Lone Ranger* on a black and white TV –
until I turned into Tonto, faithful, wild, and wise,
and Nemo became the brave and daring masked man
who saved the day, out on those savage western plains.

We didn't discuss why his mom kept vodka in a toilet tank
or why his doctor dad didn't prescribe polio shots in time.
Instead, we sneaked down the rugged old tote road
to the forbidden swamp, since Nemo could move almost
as fast as I could on his crutches or his callused knees.

I often retold our adventures aloud so we could relive them,
and Nemo became my doorway to a future filled with joy
and sorrow, where I learned that wherever we go,
we can be heroes like Tonto and the Lone Ranger,
and help each other carry burdens – and carry on.

FRED'S FOREVER FRIEND

for Frederick Manfred Junior

Every June twelfth draws me back
to the deathbed of my brother,
his lean, bronze profile on the pillow
in the pale hospice room,
sunlight blazing on the wilted red roses
outside the window.

Dust motes dance above
his scarred, long-tortured body,
and he's no longer trying to be brave
on his journey up the mountain
he climbed from the day he could walk
to the day he never walked again.

Soft music curls amid the whispers of nurses
and the flitting shadows of unseen ghosts,
all of them prepared for what will come next –
as I am not – was not – never will be.
Why should I be?

Joel, Fred's best friend, sits beside the bed,
his presence every day a reminder
of fifty years of friendship
between two men who never shared
the same politics, religion, fortune, or fate.

When he started first grade in his new town,
Fred asked, "D'you want to be my best friend?"
and Joel said, "Yes," and from then on
we cheered their baseball games, the jokes
and stories they told, the trips they took,
and the bond they shared. Even in death.

VI

THE HEDGE
GODDESS

The Hedge Goddess

ALMOST EVERY AFTERNOON Jade and I had great times riding our bicycles up and down streets named after famous writers in Palo Alto, California. We peddled up Emerson, down Hawthorne, across Homer, on and on. Jade was working on her Masters in Social Work and I was working on my Masters in English, and long, giggling bike rides were a good way to relax. But after a few weeks of neighborhood rides we realized something was missing, so one Saturday night we drove up to a party in Frisco to meet some guys.

Soon after we arrived Jade met this lifeguard with curly gold hair and a tan cheerful California face and I can't remember if they danced or just stood close to each other looking as if they wanted to dance. I introduced myself to all the other guys, one or two at a time, swallowing gin and tonics or whatever they poured into my glass and fixing my gaze on every word they said which was mostly "politics," "computers," or "sports."

Every time I glanced over at Jade she looked happier and happier. Toward the end of the party, just before I switched to beer to sober up, she sidled over and said, "Sam will take me home, so you can drive the car back, okay?"

"Sam who?"

"Sam Greenfield," she said, and grinned. "California guys are the best in bed, you know."

"I don't know," I said. "There weren't very many California guys in the small towns of Minnesota where I spent my high school years."

"Too bad for small towns in Minnesota," Jade said.

I was suddenly overwhelmed with gin-green envy. Not only was Jade going to leave the party with the golden-haired lifeguard but she was also deep into a five year relationship with another very sexy man, Seth Salvo, who had the best sense of humor on both sides of the Rockies and was avidly waiting for Jade to come and live with him, way, way, way back in Boston. "What about Seth?" I whispered.

Jade grinned for the ninety-seventh time and said, "See ya!"

I wanted some fresh air, so I went outside and climbed up on top of an eight foot tall green hedge in front of the house. I had to crawl inside the hedge first, and then wriggle up through a very narrow toothy tunnel full of sharp little twigs and pointy leaves, but I made it to the carefully-trimmed flat green top of the hedge and threw myself on my stomach before it could tilt over with my weight.

It was a wonderful change. I could see almost everyone at the party, chatting on the lawn or dancing inside the house. Slowly, carefully, I turned onto my back with my beer resting on my stomach and teetered back and forth gently with the occasional tremors of the hedge.

Some of the San Francisco stars were covered with clouds and some floated free beside the moon. I thought of my friend, Helen, who faints whenever anyone mentions how many light years we are away from the stars. The ungraspable concept of the magnificently vast universe compared to Helen herself makes her feel so dizzy that she begins to feel certain – horribly certain – that she's going to die in the next space-time instant, which, in a way, she will.

Next I thought about Seth, and how as soon as I got back East I might just tell him what Jade had been up to in California with the tall, handsome lifeguard. But then I realized that drunk or sober I'd never rat on Jade. We'd had too much fun for too many months and her loving, carefree grin can make the sorriest waif believe the world is good and time and space will last forever. Seth has always had a wonderful smile, too, but it often has a lot of black eyebrows and sadness and anger behind it, so it doesn't feel like pure water over the dam. That's probably why he's so in love with Jade – he knows she's going to come out of life with some smiles and joy no matter what.

So I swayed back and forth on the friendly, marvelous, taller-than-most-mere-mortals hedge, who seemed to have my back so far. And every time I finished my beer someone handed another beer up to me, maybe because they got a kick out of this oddball Midwestern gal hanging out on top of an eight foot hedge.

A few guys tried to climb up next to me, but as soon as they got near the top, the hedge would casually bend over and dump them off while I hung on. Two women, who were not as tall or as muscular as the guys also tried to join me, but they, too, were tossed into the darkness. It was a one woman hedge.

After awhile one guy who had abandoned his heroic effort to climb up next to me sat down under the hedge and told me his entire life story. Where he was born, what his parents were like, what he planned to do for a living, and how he was going to propose to the girl he loved even if she possibly didn't love him. He couldn't see my face and I couldn't see his, but he rambled on and on to the hedge goddess. When he left, another guy came by, and he talked even longer. His name was Father Joe Coyle, and he had a crush on a registered nurse in his parish and he couldn't decide whether or not to leave the priesthood to marry her so he could live at her side forever. I could easily see both sides of his dilemma because he so eloquently described his choices – he deeply loved his work, and he intensely loved the nurse. I knew that if it were me, I'd probably leave the priesthood for love, but I also knew I couldn't be responsible for so many beloved parishioners, not in a million years. So I lay above him, crooning, "Uh-huh, uh-huh," swaying and swooning and sipping my beer.

After Joe Coyle ambled back into the house, I met another man, Lynn Snyder, who told me how he and his wife used to belong to a religious cult in Florida, but when they became the parents of two darling sons they began to resent the fact that the cult wouldn't let them spend even their short thirty minute lunch period with the boys. They were required to eat in a cold, hard lunchroom with the other adults in the cult, and their sons had to eat in a separate cold, hard lunchroom, and they were forbidden to take the kids down to the beach after work. So they left the cult. But now none of their longtime relatives or old friends would speak to them and they sometimes woke up at night feeling as if they were only half there. If that. Lynn wondered if he should at least contact his mother, because he knew she still loved him and would always love him. But if he did contact her, what if she told the rest of the cult where he and his wife and kids were now living? "Scary," he said.

And again, I quietly said nothing more than, "Uh-huh, uh-huh," because I knew I would try to connect with my mother if I had joined a cult and then left it, but I was not Lynn Snyder and my mother was not his mother. He thanked me for listening and wandered off to find his wife and I felt loved and safe and powerful and absent all at the same time. I have no memory of how I climbed down from the hedge or how I got home.

The next day Jade told me that she remembered every moment she spent with Sam the California lifeguard, but even though I made her a pot of black coffee she wouldn't share one instant of what they did after they left the party. I told her I'd wait a long time, if I had to, to hear the whole sexy story. I figured that if she didn't want to talk about Sam right away, she'd probably feel compelled to share everything that happened with him the next time we hit a party with a hedge.

VII

A GREAT WIND

I Won't Read My Poems

for Robert and Ruth Bly

Today I feel as alone as I have ever felt,
so I won't read my poems at the funeral of my friend,

not even the verses I wrote in a tailspin
under a blessed, cursed, disappearing, re-appearing moon.

I'll shelve my midnight tears and four a.m. fears,
close my journal, put down my pen,

and struggle on without the dear one whose lifelong
dance of words we have come to celebrate.

Let his poems ripple through us like water, or wind,
and be spoken in honor of his long life,

words that remind us to write our own poems
to comfort the living and the dead for the world ahead –

in which we will die, too, but live for a while, in words.

Michaela's Poem

The first flakes of snow, as large as aspen leaves,
fall through the rust-red oaks and sturdy cedars,

and the still-rippling lake, grey and everlasting, swallows
their delicate messages and carries them away.

If these white fluttering poems from the sky
carry a word or two for you, and we who love you,

before they dissolve in what is left of summer
and every summer we have shared, what do they say?

Is it "kiss," "hug," "come back," and "don't leave"?
Or do they whisper, "sleep warm," "I love you," and "let go"?

I don't expect anything more from sky or earth today,
and I know whatever I gave or give isn't enough,

but you were, and are, a creative, loving friend,
and all your open-hearted gifts were free.

IN A DREAM MY FRIEND SAILS TOWARD ME

In a dream my friend sails toward me, smiling,
her hair grown only a few curly inches.
She says, *I know my path will be short.*

I smile back at her, blessed by this woman I love,
who can no longer talk and share with me,
since the friend she turns to now is death.

This dream is true. But nothing she has meant to me
will pass away. Her last breath will become
my first breath each time I breathe.

She'll live in my heart
the way the last wave rolls on shore
with the same unfailing rhythm as the first,

then fades away, then returns,
rejoining us again and again,
lending its voice to the planet's turning.

A GREAT WIND

She tells me she's shocked she hasn't longer to live.

Helpless in the face of my dying friend
I can't find the strength to pour a glass of water.

Dark clouds unravel across the autumn sky
and a great wind blows dead leaves high and wide
over trees and roof tops, and into our open front door.

I stand outside, free but never free,
waiting to be claimed by wind in all its rambling glory,
wind from every direction,
wind that flows within me like blood inside my veins,
like the spirit of my friend.

Wind forever with me, now.

A Dying Friend

My greatest fear is that I will die now, too.

I feel my body is joined with hers
ever since we met beside the ancient river
to speak our griefs and joys,
to whisper our failures and fears,
to summon our hopes and dreams, our work and play,
our family and friends, living and dead.

We no longer meet to share our songs,
in this too-often lonely world,
where we were grateful to find each other –
just as we were, whoever we were –
happy to honor that lucky day
when we first sat down together, and found a friend.

STRIPPED BARE

My friend died last night at twenty past ten,
but I only found out this morning.

I open the oven door, but it won't warm the house.
I listen to the wind, which tells me nothing I want to know.

How far must I travel before I find a friend who makes me
feel so close to who I am and whoever I hope to be?

How long before I dare to feel what I'm missing?
I don't feel love coming toward me or from me.

I feel as if I can't love anyone. I'm stripped bare.

I try to summon her face, her voice, her touch –
but she's not here and I know it.

Yes, there we were, and there she was, but now she's not.
And my body cannot lie.

Anxiety in Five Parts

1.
Anxiety is an unwelcome surprise, a chasm
that suddenly opens, too wide to leap,
like the loss of a purse that holds our phone and keys,
everything that connects us to those we love,
to who we were, and are, and hope to be.

2.
Anxiety is a maelstrom of moans and shouts buried in our flesh
when we struggle to keep our pain silent,
a thorn that cuts more deeply when no one pulls it out.

3.
Anxiety is a cross on which we crucify ourselves
when we believe we must suffer for our sins.
But when and where were those sins born?
Were we too young and small to survive the flood,
feed the multitudes, or rise from the dead?
Why weren't we taught how to survive
the crashing death of hope?

4.
Anxiety is a nightmare with no way out,
whether we're asleep or awake –
and if we can't embrace it,
our best friends can become our enemies,
or we can become an enemy to ourselves.

5.
Anxiety strikes when we don't know
what we fear or how to stop that fear,
and we can't retrace our steps
to where some part of us we left behind
waits to welcome us with open arms.

ENTERING THE MAZE

I can't grasp, unravel, describe,
      or understand death.
What lies beyond me is a maze I enter,
      but can never leave.

My heart's drumbeat drives
      the lifting and setting down of my feet,
until my breath joins in and sings,
      "Keep dancing."

No one I know has ever finished the dance
      into the unknown and returned.
But a voice that feels solid and certain
      tells me, "Keep dancing."

A Sister's Farewell

for Marya Manfred

When she was not asleep, away in the music
she'd heard every day since she was born,
she spoke, and she sang, often alone,
in the room with the oxygen, the drugs,
and the oak tree outside, empty of leaves.

She spoke and sang to friends and family,
playmates and workmates, living and dead.
And some said she spoke and sang to the angels
beside her bed – and others said she wasn't
surrounded by angels at all, being enough
of an angel herself, to those who loved her most.

Yes, she spoke and sang, and what mattered
is that she heard what she said and sang.
Yes, she listened, as the fine musician she was,
to her own unique, living, dying, true voice,
as part of earth's music, its rhythm, and its dream.

With the Dead at Blue Mound

I walk alone across the winter prairie,
wind-whipped and cold to the bone,
every grass blade and flower buried in ice.

The spirits of my dead mother and brother
rise from the snowy earth and flow with me,
dark, deep, and certain as sorrow.

And the spirits of my dead father and sister
stride before me and behind me, untamed
as the bright, blue-singing sky.

Like the flesh-colored quartzite rocks
rubbed smooth by generations of bison,
I'm full of blood, my heart steady.

I can walk east to the sun, west to the moon,
south to the slow-running river,
and north to the land of the white bear's roar.

Here on the prairie all directions lead home,
and I do not stop because I cannot stop,
on my past, present, and future journey.

IF THE DEAD COULD VOTE

> *Dead people. So dead people voted, and I think the*
> *number is close to 5,000 people.*
> — Donald Trump

If the dead could vote, no one could stop them,
whether they flew down from heaven or rose up from hell.

Their voices would sound like wind
flowing through our hustling streets and hushed valleys.

Most of us would not see them until we're near death,
or preparing to emerge from our mother's womb.

Whatever our votes might be, even if we all agree,
the dead would easily outnumber us, and win.

They might vote to send us back to our birthright,
to the truth of human loneliness and passion,

and the gift of living in a land we love
that lies between what we make of heaven, or of hell.

How to Frighten the Dead

Don't die. The dead want us to stay alive.

Don't over-eat, over-spend, over-worry,
over-control everyone you hate or love,
even those who want what isn't yours to give.

Don't listen when your dead family or friends
beg you for less noise, less greed, less pain,
less loss of heart, or head, or hands.

Don't tell them you've forgotten they're still part of you,
or how shocked and frightened you felt as they died,
helpless to ease their journey, or your own.

Remember that a piece of you dies every day
you can't accept your grief about what's missing
from your life – the sweet bond you shared with them.

Then wait for your daily dream of living long and well
to swim in with the tide. This will not frighten them.
And you don't want to scare them away.

Saying Goodbye to What I Fear Most

If I could say goodbye to what I fear most
my breath would flow, calm, like mist over water,

windows and doors would open,
and new paths would lead in all directions.

I would thank everyone and everything for *being*,
as mysterious as breath or blood or bone.

People, animals, plants, or stones could rely on me,
just as I could rely on them.

Many of those I love might die,
but I would lie down beside them to learn the way.

And when I die I would dissolve into the throbbing
web of stars that gave birth to me

when I first said goodbye to what I fear most.

Against My Will I Felt a Flowering

Against my will I felt a flowering
in some deep forgotten place
as the stars arched toward dawn,
a softening of body, of soul,
a traveling voice without sound
that told me to open gently, to embrace
myself and everyone and everything,
to ride each unexpected wind,
and greet each passing grain of sand,
drop of water, or rising flame.

This journey we take is a dance
that began before our birth
and will go on after our death,
all of us part of rock, wave, web,
and whisper, until even willpower
becomes a part of what will be –
but without the forever fear of dying
or being lost in the ravenous terror
of never having been here at all.

THE RISING MOON SPEAKS TO ME

My life revealed itself to me last night
    in one long sleepless journey
as if it were a story told by the rising moon,
    born in the eastern sky, then flowing west
to descend and die with the morning light.

I saw a girl explore her world on a sailing ship,
    a giant fallen elm in an emerald sea of trees.
I saw her work and play, at home, in school,
    saving for a car she learned to drive
from coast to coast and down the Mississippi.

I watched her turn into a flower, a tree, a horse,
    a meadowlark, even a dolphin,
those gods of land and sky she most admired,
    whose roots, hooves, wings, fins, and brains
sang to her with words she heard in dreams.

I saw her write poems, memoirs, and stories,
    fact and fiction, since both were true.
I saw her meet new friends and fall in love
    with the dear man she married,
who helped her raise their iridescent children.

And at the end of the moon's long arc
    I saw a woman who would die, like everyone,
and I cried like a newborn, floating once more
    in the ocean of suns, moons, and stars.
I cried for the beauty and truth of what has been,
    what is, and what must be.

VIII

THREE FEET UNDER

Three Feet Under

Tom and I spent the first four days of our honeymoon in a farm house on the Missouri River lent to us by my old friends Sam and Grete. Then we headed west toward California with Margie and Mel, two friends from Boston who wanted to see the Black Hills.

After a long day of tramping through the Badlands we stopped for burgers and beer at a roadside bar in the middle of the prairie east of Deadwood. Tom and Margie and Mel started a conversation about space and time and destiny and civilization, while I wandered outside to feed an apple to a lone horse grazing in a corral behind the bar.

An hour later they came out of the bar, talking about life and death and the fate of the human race. I listened very carefully and mindfully to every word, but I couldn't find a thing to say. We drove on the winding, uphill, downhill road until the sky turned rose-red and then dark purple and we all agreed to stop and find a place to sleep on the prairie.

We slowed down, looking for a good spot to spread our sleeping bags. Our car crept past herds of grazing deer and a startled jackrabbit or two until we came to a large fenced area where a herd of bison stood like giant boulders staring west into the last vestige of the sunset. The open, unfenced prairie surrounded the bison, tall bronzed grasses reaching toward a newly risen full moon the color of honey. We pulled off the road and bumped across a hummocky field and parked.

Tom and I dragged our sleeping bags from the car and tucked ourselves away on one side of a sloping hill, and Margie and Mel laid out their sleeping bags about fifty feet away. Tom and I tried to zip our bags together, but after fumbling around for awhile we gave up and fell asleep next to each other in separate bags.

Half an hour later, coming out of a dead sleep, I heard voices. I propped myself up on one elbow and saw a black and white police car pulled up next to our car with both its front doors open and a static-voice from a two-way radio bristling into the darkness. Two officers with flashlights stood next to their open doors, flashing their beams past us several times before they pinpointed our sleeping bags.

I jumped up and stepped into my sandals and went down to talk with them.

The officers' voices were razor-sharp and suspicious as I stumbled toward them, half asleep, reaching out to take hold of some sagebrush, a wispy tobacco plant, a spindly baby tree, anything that was on my path, straining to get back into the waking world.

When I reached the police car the shorter officer frowned at me and the taller officer said, "Hello there!"

"Hello," I said.

"So ... What-er you folks doing out here?" he asked.

"Sleeping ..." I stammered. "We were driving and we got tired and ..."

The shorter officer interrupted. "Not here! You don't sleep on State Park ground. It's illegal!"

"I'm sorry," I said. "We didn't know it was illegal and we didn't want to drive any farther in the dark."

The taller officer grunted. "How many of you are there?"

"Me and my husband and two friends."

"Where you from, then?"

"I'm from Minnesota, and Tom's from New Jersey, and my friends are from Boston. They've never seen South Dakota, not even the Black Hills." The tall one threw the light of his flashlight across the grass until he spotlighted Tom's pale white face staring out of his sleeping bag, and then the two even paler white faces of Margie and Mel. I felt suddenly ticked off at all three of them. Why didn't they come down and help me talk with the police?

The short officer gestured, "You guys can camp up the road a ways at the campground. But this is State Park land."

"How far up the road?" I asked.

"Mebbe twenty," he said.

I sighed, and the tall officer said, "It's a ways."

"Yes," I said.

He shrugged. "So … I tell ya what. You folks go ahead and sleep here tonight, but you gotta get out by dawn or the guys on the next shift will be pissed 'cause we let you stay. And don't make it a practice to sleep in areas that aren't designated for camping. It's dangerous."

"I'm sorry," I said. I waved at the hills. "What sort of danger should we look out for, out here?"

He paused and looked at the short officer and the short officer looked at him. Finally the tall one said, "Well, there's coyotes, but I s'pose they're more scared of us than we are of them."

"There's cactus all over the place," the short one said. "Takes days and weeks to get prickly pear outta your skin. Point is, you never know what's gonna come along – see what I mean?"

"Sure," I said. "But there haven't been any murders, have there? Or robberies?"

"You mean two-footed trouble," the tall one said. "Nope."

He looked at the short one, who said, "Nope."

The tall one turned off his flashlight and looked around, at the looming moon, at the Black Hills hulking in the distance, at the huffing bison in their enclosure, and then he spit with great satisfaction into the wind and watched it float past the three of us and land in the dirt about ten feet away. He grinned at his partner. "What a job," he said.

"Yep," the short one smiled. He turned off his flashlight and pulled out a pack of Chesterfields and offered one to me and when I shook my head he lit one up for himself. "Can't believe they pay us."

The tall one set one foot clad with a dusty black police boot up on a nearby rock and cocked his head to look up at the stars. "Yep, I feel like a bank robber," he said. Then he gave the short cop a thumbs up sign, and they slipped into their squad car and bumped off across the prairie grass to the road, where they flicked their headlights a few times to say goodbye and drove rapidly away.

I walked through heavy dew to the sleeping bags and announced, "It's okay. We can stay." But Tom and Margie and Mel knew that because they were tucked back in their sleeping bags already, heads covered, maybe even sound asleep.

I crawled in and tugged my zipper up to my chin and laid there and stared up at the moon. The bison in the nearby enclosure huffed out, out, out.

I never heard the bison breathe in, though I waited, and after awhile I closed my eyes – and whether or not I was still awake I felt the earth pull at the whole length of my body. The prairie opened up and drew me in until I was lying about three feet under the surface, cradled as if I were in a mother's or father's arms. The suck of the earth was so intent and palpable, I thought for a moment that maybe I should wrestle or struggle my way back up to grass level again or I'd never get out. But after another moment, I decided to let go. My face, my arms and legs, my chest, my spine, went soft, and I thought, half-awake: if death is like this, I'll die gladly.

When I woke at dawn I was still three feet under-ground, eyes closed, safe and warm. And when I was ready, the earth gave a shove between my shoulder blades and against the back of my thighs and pushed me back up like a mouth thrusting forth a tongue. My eyes opened, and blinked into the sun, and I knew what the earth had given me that night. It was space and time and destiny and civi-lization and life and death and the fate of the human race – all rolled into one. But without the words.

Freya Manfred is a longtime Midwesterner who has lived on both coasts. She attended Macalester College and Stanford University, and has received a Radcliffe Grant and a National Endowment for the Arts Grant. Her seventh collection, *Swimming With A Hundred Year Old Snapping Turtle*, won the 2009 Midwest Booksellers Choice Award for Poetry, and her poems have appeared in more than a hundred reviews and magazines and more than fifty anthologies. Her memoir, *Frederick Manfred: A Daughter Remembers*, was nominated for a Minnesota Book Award and an Iowa Historical Society Award. Her more recent memoir is *Raising Twins: A True Life Adventure*. She lives with her husband, screenwriter Thomas Pope, in Stillwater, Minnesota. Their sons, visual artists Bly Pope and Rowan Pope, have illustrated many of her books.

Additional information is available on Freya's website at www. freyamanfredwriter.com.